# ONE DAY AT A TIME
( a guided journal )

Copyright Emily Byrnes

2018

# ALSO BY EMILY BYRNES:

**Guided Journals:**

*One Breath at a Time (a guided journal for anxiety)*

*One Page at a Time (a blank journal)*

**Poetry:**

*Things I Learned in the Night*

*Swim*

*A Strangely Wrapped Gift*

# Reasons to journal:

Get organized-track mood-get healthy-destress-stay hydrated-set goals-stay motivated-track sleep-remember meds-stay inspired-it's therapeutic-collect quotes-budget track-self-love-self-care-set priorities-make time for you-decompress-be more mindful-have a creative outlet-make a little space in your world-be in the present-reflect-plan-schedule-unplug-track habits-stay inspired-develop healthy coping skills-find some headspace-take notes-stay positive-see the bigger picture-keep track of important things-keep a dream log-make to-do lists-track symptoms-make something pretty out of nothing-stay kind-remember important things-observe growth.

# Things to know: Line Graphs

In this guided journal, *Line graphs* are used as anxiety trackers. (*Who knew math would actually come in handy?*) You will see this exact chart every now and then in the journal, and it is useful because it allows you to see patterns. For myself, I noticed I am usually the most anxious at night.

Anxiety levels:

Line graph example:

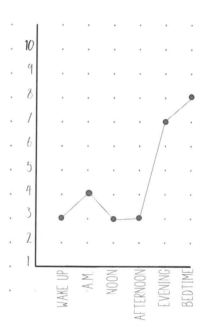

# Things to know: Bar Graphs

Bar graphs are super easy and great for marking progress. You will see a few examples of these in this journal used for to-do lists and hydration tracking, but you can make a bar graph for just about anything! (sleep, nutrients, savings, etc.) Here is an example of a bar graph and how it works:

## To-do list:

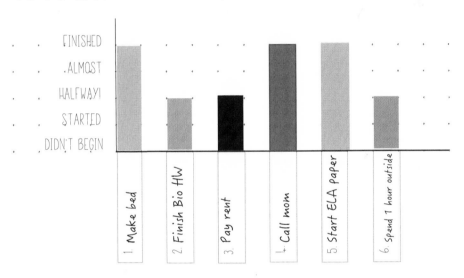

(Feel free to get colorful or stick to a more minimalist look with black and white.)

Hello, sunshine

she believed she could,

so she did.

Week of __/__/__ - __/__/__

GOAL FOR THE WEEK:

_____

Date: ___/___/_____

TODAY'S GOAL: _____

## To-do list:

| | |
|---|---|
| FINISHED | |
| .ALMOST | |
| HALFWAY! | |
| STARTED | |
| DIDN'T BEGIN | |

1    2    3    4    5    6

## Self-care Checklist:

☐ STAY HYDRATED
☐ EAT A HEALTHY BREAKFAST
☐ TAKE MEDS
☐ SPEND TIME IN NATURE
☐ SHOWER/BATHE
☐ EAT LOTS OF PLANTS
☐ READ
☐ EXERCISE
☐ RANDOM ACT OF KINDNESS
☐ ENJOY A HOT DRINK
☐ UNPLUG FOR AN HOUR
☐ YOGA/MEDITATION/MINDFULNESS

## Anxiety levels:

10
9
8
7
6
5
4
3
2
1

WAKE UP   A.M.   NOON   AFTERNOON   EVENING   BEDTIME

Date: ___/___/_____

TODAY'S GOAL: _____

TO DO LIST:

- 

- 

- 

. . . . . . . . . . . . . . . . . . . . . . . . . . . . . . . . . . . . . . . . . . . . . . . . . . . . . . . . . . .

SELF-CARE CHECKLIST                    3 good things:

- [ ] STAY HYDRATED
- [ ] EAT A HEALTHY BREAKFAST            1.
- [ ] TAKE MEDS
- [ ] SPEND TIME IN NATURE
- [ ] SHOWER/BATHE                       2.
- [ ] EAT LOTS OF PLANTS
- [ ] READ
- [ ] EXERCISE
- [ ] RANDOM ACT OF KINDNESS             3.
- [ ] ENJOY A HOT DRINK
- [ ] UNPLUG FOR AN HOUR
- [ ] YOGA/MEDITATION/
      PRACTICE MINDFULNESS

. . . . . . . . . . . . . . . . . . . . . . . . . . . . . . . . . . . . . . . . . . . . . . . . . . . . . . . . . . .

Describe your identity:

Date: ___/___/_____

TODAY'S GOAL: _____

To-do list:

○

○

○

Self-care checklist:

☐ STAY HYDRATED
☐ EAT A HEALTHY BREAKFAST
☐ TAKE MEDS
☐ SPEND TIME IN NATURE
☐ SHOWER/BATHE
☐ EAT LOTS OF PLANTS!
☐ READ
☐ EXERCISE
☐ RANDOM ACT OF KINDNESS
☐ UNPLUG FOR AN HOUR
☐ YOGA/MEDITATION

(WORK YOUR MAGIC)

Date: ___/___/_____

TODAY'S GOAL: _____

Doodle something pretty:

SELF-CARE CHECKLIST:

☐ STAY HYDRATED
☐ EAT A HEALTHY BREAKFAST
☐ TAKE MEDS
☐ SPEND TIME IN NATURE
☐ SHOWER/BATHE
☐ EAT LOTS OF PLANTS
☐ READ
☐ EXERCISE
☐ RANDOM ACT OF KINDNESS
☐ ENJOY A HOT DRINK
☐ UNPLUG FOR AN HOUR
☐ YOGA/MEDITATION/MINDFULNES

HYDRATION LOG (WATER ONLY!)

fluid ounces

100 +
.90
.80
.70
.60
.50
.40
.30
.20
.10
0

(don't forget a reusable bottle!)

DATE: ____/____/_____

#1 GOAL: _____

To-do list key: (fill in with colors/textures of your choosing, then complete box-chart!)

☐ started  ☐ finished  ☐ forgot  ☐ push to tomorrow

Tasks:
→

1. 2. 3. 4. 5. 6. 7.

a.m.

afternoon

p.m.

# FOOD DIARY:

BREAKFAST: _____

LUNCH: _____

DINNER: _____

SNACKS:_____

WATER (OZ/ML):_____

# SPACE

"rain, come see me.

we got things to grow."

-r. iver

Week of __/__/__ - __/__/__

GOAL FOR THE WEEK:

_____

Date: ___/___/_____

TODAY'S GOAL: _____

## To-do list:

|  | | | | | | |
|---|---|---|---|---|---|---|
| FINISHED | | | | | | |
| .ALMOST | | | | | | |
| HALFWAY! | | | | | | |
| STARTED | | | | | | |
| DIDN'T BEGIN | | | | | | |
| | 1 | 2 | 3 | 4 | 5 | 6 |

## Self-care Checklist:

☐ STAY HYDRATED
☐ EAT A HEALTHY BREAKFAST
☐ TAKE MEDS
☐ SPEND TIME IN NATURE
☐ SHOWER/BATHE
☐ EAT LOTS OF PLANTS
☐ READ
☐ EXERCISE
☐ RANDOM ACT OF KINDNESS
☐ ENJOY A HOT DRINK
☐ UNPLUG FOR AN HOUR
☐ YOGA/MEDITATION/MINDFULNESS

## Anxiety levels:

10
9
8
7
6
5
4
3
2
1

WAKE UP | A.M. | NOON | AFTERNOON | EVENING | BEDTIME

Date: ___/___/_____

TODAY'S GOAL: _____

TO DO LIST:

- 
- 
- 

SELF-CARE CHECKLIST

*3 good things:*

- ☐ STAY HYDRATED
- ☐ EAT A HEALTHY BREAKFAST
- ☐ TAKE MEDS
- ☐ SPEND TIME IN NATURE
- ☐ SHOWER/BATHE
- ☐ EAT LOTS OF PLANTS
- ☐ READ
- ☐ EXERCISE
- ☐ RANDOM ACT OF KINDNESS
- ☐ ENJOY A HOT DRINK
- ☐ UNPLUG FOR AN HOUR
- ☐ YOGA/MEDITATION/ PRACTICE MINDFULNESS

1.

2.

3.

*How are you feeling about yourself today?*

Date: ___/___/_____

TODAY'S GOAL: _____

To-do list:

○

○

○

(WORK YOUR MAGIC)

Self-care checklist:

☐ STAY HYDRATED

☐ EAT A HEALTHY BREAKFAST

☐ TAKE MEDS

☐ SPEND TIME IN NATURE

☐ SHOWER/BATHE

☐ EAT LOTS OF PLANTS!

☐ READ

☐ EXERCISE

☐ RANDOM ACT OF KINDNESS

☐ UNPLUG FOR AN HOUR

☐ YOGA/MEDITATION

Date: ___/___/_____

TODAY'S GOAL: _____

Doodle something pretty:

SELF-CARE CHECKLIST:

☐ STAY HYDRATED
☐ EAT A HEALTHY BREAKFAST
☐ TAKE MEDS
☐ SPEND TIME IN NATURE
☐ SHOWER/BATHE
☐ EAT LOTS OF PLANTS
☐ READ
☐ EXERCISE
☐ RANDOM ACT OF KINDNESS
☐ ENJOY A HOT DRINK
☐ UNPLUG FOR AN HOUR
☐ YOGA/MEDITATION/MINDFULNES

HYDRATION LOG (WATER ONLY!)

fluid ounces

100 +
.90
.80
.70
.60
.50
.40
.30
.20
.10
0

DATE: ____/____/_____

#1 GOAL: _____

---

To-do list key: (fill in with colors/textures of your choosing, then complete box-chart!)

☐ started          ☐ finished          ☐ forgot          ☐ push to tomorrow

---

Tasks:
→

|           | 1. | 2. | 3. | 4. | 5. | 6. | 7. |
|-----------|----|----|----|----|----|----|----|
| a.m.      |    |    |    |    |    |    |    |
| afternoon |    |    |    |    |    |    |    |
| p.m.      |    |    |    |    |    |    |    |

# FOOD DIARY:

BREAKFAST: _____

LUNCH: _____

DINNER: _____

SNACKS: _____

WATER (OZ/ML): _____

# SPACE

"DON'T LET ANYONE TELL YOU
THERE ISN'T STRENGTH IN BEING SOFT.
THE OCEAN CARVED OUT THE WORLD,
BUT IT CAN STILL CARRY YOU

ANYWHERE"

-LEAH J STONE

Week of __/__/__ - __/__/__

GOAL FOR THE WEEK:

_____

Date: ___/___/_____

TODAY'S GOAL: _____

# To-do list:

| | | |
|---|---|---|
| FINISHED | | |
| .ALMOST | | |
| HALFWAY! | | |
| STARTED | | |
| .DIDN'T BEGIN | | |

1  2  3  4  5  6

## Self-care Checklist:

- ☐ STAY HYDRATED
- ☐ EAT A HEALTHY BREAKFAST
- ☐ TAKE MEDS
- ☐ SPEND TIME IN NATURE
- ☐ SHOWER/BATHE
- ☐ EAT LOTS OF PLANTS
- ☐ READ
- ☐ EXERCISE
- ☐ RANDOM ACT OF KINDNESS
- ☐ ENJOY A HOT DRINK
- ☐ UNPLUG FOR AN HOUR
- ☐ YOGA/MEDITATION/MINDFULNESS

## Anxiety levels:

10
9
8
7
6
5
4
3
2
1

WAKE UP  A.M.  NOON  AFTERNOON  EVENING  BEDTIME

Date: ___/___/_____

TODAY'S GOAL: _____

TO DO LIST:

- 

- 

- 

SELF-CARE CHECKLIST

3 good things:

☐ STAY HYDRATED
☐ EAT A HEALTHY BREAKFAST          1.
☐ TAKE MEDS
☐ SPEND TIME IN NATURE
☐ SHOWER/BATHE                     2.
☐ EAT LOTS OF PLANTS
☐ READ
☐ EXERCISE
☐ RANDOM ACT OF KINDNESS           3.
☐ ENJOY A HOT DRINK
☐ UNPLUG FOR AN HOUR
☐ YOGA/MEDITATION/
   PRACTICE MINDFULNESS

mountains or ocean? beach day or sightseeing? cats or dogs?

Date: ___/___/_____

TODAY'S GOAL: _____

To-do list:

○

○

○

Self-care checklist:

☐ STAY HYDRATED

☐ EAT A HEALTHY BREAKFAST

☐ TAKE MEDS

☐ SPEND TIME IN NATURE

☐ SHOWER/BATHE

☐ EAT LOTS OF PLANTS!

☐ READ

☐ EXERCISE

☐ RANDOM ACT OF KINDNESS

☐ UNPLUG FOR AN HOUR

☐ YOGA/MEDITATION

(WORK YOUR MAGIC)

Date: ___/___/_____

TODAY'S GOAL: _____

To Do List:

○

○

○

Mood Tracker:

AM:

Mid-Day:

PM:

Inspiring Quote: _____
_____

SELF-CARE CHECKLIST:

☐ STAY HYDRATED
☐ EAT A HEALTHY BREAKFAST
☐ TAKE MEDS
☐ SPEND TIME IN NATURE
☐ SHOWER/BATHE
☐ EAT LOTS OF PLANTS
☐ READ
☐ EXERCISE
☐ RANDOM ACT OF KINDNESS
☐ ENJOY A HOT DRINK
☐ UNPLUG FOR AN HOUR
☐ YOGA/MEDITATION/MINDFULNES

HYDRATION LOG (WATER ONLY!)

Fluid ounces

100 +
.90
.80
.70
.60
.50
.40
.30
.20
.10
0

(don't forget a reusable bottle!)

DATE: ___/___/_____

#1 GOAL: _____

---

To-do list key: (fill in with colors/textures of your choosing, then complete box-chart!)

☐ started        ☐ finished        ☐ forgot        ☐ push to tomorrow

---

Tasks:
→

1.   2.   3.   4.   5.   6.   7.

|          |   |   |   |   |   |   |   |
|----------|---|---|---|---|---|---|---|
| a.m.     |   |   |   |   |   |   |   |
| afternoon|   |   |   |   |   |   |   |
| p.m.     |   |   |   |   |   |   |   |

## FOOD DIARY:

BREAKFAST: _____

LUNCH: _____

DINNER: _____

SNACKS: _____

WATER (OZ/ML): _____

SPACE

"do not be afraid
-TO OUTGROW-
the ones who
DO NOT WATER YOU"

-EMILY BYRNES

Week of __/__/__ - __/__/__

GOAL FOR THE WEEK:

_____

Date: ___/___/_____

TODAY'S GOAL: _____

## To-do list:

FINISHED

.ALMOST

HALFWAY!

STARTED

.DIDN'T BEGIN

1  2  3  4  5  6

## Self-care Checklist:

☐ STAY HYDRATED
☐ EAT A HEALTHY BREAKFAST
☐ TAKE MEDS
☐ SPEND TIME IN NATURE
☐ SHOWER/BATHE
☐ EAT LOTS OF PLANTS
☐ READ
☐ EXERCISE
☐ RANDOM ACT OF KINDNESS
☐ ENJOY A HOT DRINK
☐ UNPLUG FOR AN HOUR
☐ YOGA/MEDITATION/MINDFULNESS

## Anxiety levels:

10
9
8
7
6
5
4
3
2
1

WAKE UP   A.M.   NOON   AFTERNOON   EVENING   BEDTIME

Date: ___/___/_____

TODAY'S GOAL: _____

TO DO LIST:

- 
- 
- 

SELF-CARE CHECKLIST

*3 good things:*

☐ STAY HYDRATED
☐ EAT A HEALTHY BREAKFAST          1.
☐ TAKE MEDS
☐ SPEND TIME IN NATURE
☐ SHOWER/BATHE                     2.
☐ EAT LOTS OF PLANTS
☐ READ
☐ EXERCISE
☐ RANDOM ACT OF KINDNESS           3
☐ ENJOY A HOT DRINK
☐ UNPLUG FOR AN HOUR
☐ YOGA/MEDITATION/
   PRACTICE MINDFULNESS

*People I've loved:*

Date: ___/___/_____

To-do list:

○

○

○

Self-care checklist:

☐ STAY HYDRATED

☐ EAT A HEALTHY BREAKFAST

☐ TAKE MEDS

☐ SPEND TIME IN NATURE

☐ SHOWER/BATHE

☐ EAT LOTS OF PLANTS!

☐ READ

☐ EXERCISE

☐ RANDOM ACT OF KINDNESS

☐ UNPLUG FOR AN HOUR

☐ YOGA/MEDITATION

(WORK YOUR MAGIC)

Date: ___/___/_____

TODAY'S GOAL: _____

Doodle something pretty:

SELF-CARE CHECKLIST:

☐ STAY HYDRATED
☐ EAT A HEALTHY BREAKFAST
☐ TAKE MEDS
☐ SPEND TIME IN NATURE
☐ SHOWER/BATHE
☐ EAT LOTS OF PLANTS
☐ READ
☐ EXERCISE
☐ RANDOM ACT OF KINDNESS
☐ ENJOY A HOT DRINK
☐ UNPLUG FOR AN HOUR
☐ YOGA/MEDITATION/MINDFULNES

HYDRATION LOG (WATER ONLY!)

Fluid ounces

100 +
.90
.80
.70
.60
.50
.40
.30
.20
.10
0

DATE: ___/___/_____

#1 GOAL: _____

| To-do list key: (fill in with colors/textures of your choosing, then complete box-chart!) |
| ☐ started ☐ finished ☐ forgot ☐ push to |

Tasks:
→

| | 1. | 2. | 3. | 4. | 5. | 6. | 7. |
|---|---|---|---|---|---|---|---|
| a.m. | | | | | | | |
| afternoon | | | | | | | |
| p.m. | | | | | | | |

# FOOD DIARY:

BREAKFAST: _____

LUNCH: _____

DINNER: _____

SNACKS:_____

WATER (OZ/ML):_____

# S P A C E

BE KIND,
STAY HAPPY,
AND **LOVE**
WHOEVER THE HELL
SETS YOUR SOUL
ON FIRE.

-A.N. MOORE

Week of __/__/__ - __/__/__

GOAL FOR THE WEEK:

_____

Date: ___/___/_____

TODAY'S GOAL: _____

## To-do list:

FINISHED
.ALMOST
HALFWAY!
STARTED
. DIDN'T BEGIN

1  2  3  4  5  6

## Self-care Checklist:

☐ STAY HYDRATED
☐ EAT A HEALTHY BREAKFAST
☐ TAKE MEDS
☐ SPEND TIME IN NATURE
☐ SHOWER/BATHE
☐ EAT LOTS OF PLANTS
☐ READ
☐ EXERCISE
☐ RANDOM ACT OF KINDNESS
☐ ENJOY A HOT DRINK
☐ UNPLUG FOR AN HOUR
☐ YOGA/MEDITATION/MINDFULNESS

## Anxiety levels:

10
9
8
7
6
5
4
3
2
1

WAKE UP  A.M.  NOON  AFTERNOON  EVENING  BEDTIME

Date: ___/___/_____

TODAY'S GOAL: _____

## TO DO LIST:

- 
- 
- 

## SELF-CARE CHECKLIST

☐ STAY HYDRATED
☐ EAT A HEALTHY BREAKFAST
☐ TAKE MEDS
☐ SPEND TIME IN NATURE
☐ SHOWER/BATHE
☐ EAT LOTS OF PLANTS
☐ READ
☐ EXERCISE
☐ RANDOM ACT OF KINDNESS
☐ ENJOY A HOT DRINK
☐ UNPLUG FOR AN HOUR
☐ YOGA/MEDITATION/
   PRACTICE MINDFULNESS

*3 good things:*

1.

2.

3.

*Things that make you happy:*

Date: ___/___/_____

TODAY'S GOAL: _____

To-do list:

○

○

○

Self-care checklist:

☐ STAY HYDRATED

☐ EAT A HEALTHY BREAKFAST

☐ TAKE MEDS

☐ SPEND TIME IN NATURE

☐ SHOWER/BATHE

☐ EAT LOTS OF PLANTS!

☐ READ

☐ EXERCISE

☐ RANDOM ACT OF KINDNESS

☐ UNPLUG FOR AN HOUR

☐ YOGA/MEDITATION

(WORK YOUR MAGIC)

**Date:** ___/___/_____

TODAY'S GOAL: _____

To Do List:

○

○

○

Mood Tracker:

AM:

Mid-Day:

PM:

Inspiring Quote:_____

_____

SELF-CARE CHECKLIST:

HYDRATION LOG (WATER ONLY!)

☐ STAY HYDRATED
☐ EAT A HEALTHY BREAKFAST
☐ TAKE MEDS
☐ SPEND TIME IN NATURE
☐ SHOWER/BATHE
☐ EAT LOTS OF PLANTS
☐ READ
☐ EXERCISE
☐ RANDOM ACT OF KINDNESS
☐ ENJOY A HOT DRINK
☐ UNPLUG FOR AN HOUR
☐ YOGA/MEDITATION/MINDFULNES

Fluid ounces

100 +
.90
.80
.70
.60
.50
.40
.30
.20
.10
0

(don't forget a reusable bottle!)

DATE: ___/___/_____

#1 GOAL: _____

---

To-do list key: (fill in with colors/textures of your choosing, then complete box-chart!)

☐ started      ☐ finished      ☐ forgot      ☐ push to tomorrow

---

Tasks:
→

1.　2.　3.　4.　5.　6.　7.

|  | | | | | | | | | | | | | |
|---|---|---|---|---|---|---|---|---|---|---|---|---|---|
| a.m. | | | | | | | | | | | | | |
| afternoon | | | | | | | | | | | | | |
| p.m. | | | | | | | | | | | | | |

# FOOD DIARY:

BREAKFAST: _____

LUNCH: _____

DINNER: _____

SNACKS: _____

WATER (OZ/ML): _____

# SPACE

"SOMETIMES, ALL THAT MATTERS IS THAT YOU'RE *STILL TRYING*."

-WILDER

Week of __/__/__ - __/__/__

GOAL FOR THE WEEK:

_____

Date: ___/___/_____

TODAY'S GOAL: _____

## To-do list:

| | FINISHED |
| | .ALMOST |
| | HALFWAY! |
| | STARTED |
| | DIDN'T BEGIN |

1  2  3  4  5  6

## Self-care Checklist:

☐ STAY HYDRATED
☐ EAT A HEALTHY BREAKFAST
☐ TAKE MEDS
☐ SPEND TIME IN NATURE
☐ SHOWER/BATHE
☐ EAT LOTS OF PLANTS
☐ READ
☐ EXERCISE
☐ RANDOM ACT OF KINDNESS
☐ ENJOY A HOT DRINK
☐ UNPLUG FOR AN HOUR
☐ YOGA/MEDITATION/MINDFULNESS

## Anxiety levels:

10
9
8
7
6
5
4
3
2
1

WAKE UP | A.M. | NOON | AFTERNOON | EVENING | BEDTIME

Date: ___/___/_____

TODAY'S GOAL: _____

## TO DO LIST:

- 
- 
- 

## SELF-CARE CHECKLIST

3 good things:

- ☐ STAY HYDRATED
- ☐ EAT A HEALTHY BREAKFAST    1.
- ☐ TAKE MEDS
- ☐ SPEND TIME IN NATURE
- ☐ SHOWER/BATHE    2.
- ☐ EAT LOTS OF PLANTS
- ☐ READ
- ☐ EXERCISE
- ☐ RANDOM ACT OF KINDNESS    3.
- ☐ ENJOY A HOT DRINK
- ☐ UNPLUG FOR AN HOUR
- ☐ YOGA/MEDITATION/
  PRACTICE MINDFULNESS

Things that make you sad:

Date: ___/___/_____

TODAY'S GOAL: _____

To-do list:

○

○

○

Self-care checklist:

☐ STAY HYDRATED

☐ EAT A HEALTHY BREAKFAST

☐ TAKE MEDS

☐ SPEND TIME IN NATURE

☐ SHOWER/BATHE

☐ EAT LOTS OF PLANTS!

☐ READ

☐ EXERCISE

☐ RANDOM ACT OF KINDNESS

☐ UNPLUG FOR AN HOUR

☐ YOGA/MEDITATION

(WORK YOUR MAGIC)

Date: ___/___/_____

Doodle something pretty:

## SELF-CARE CHECKLIST:

☐ STAY HYDRATED
☐ EAT A HEALTHY BREAKFAST
☐ TAKE MEDS
☐ SPEND TIME IN NATURE
☐ SHOWER/BATHE
☐ EAT LOTS OF PLANTS
☐ READ
☐ EXERCISE
☐ RANDOM ACT OF KINDNESS
☐ ENJOY A HOT DRINK
☐ UNPLUG FOR AN HOUR
☐ YOGA/MEDITATION/MINDFULNES

## HYDRATION LOG (WATER ONLY!)

Fluid ounces

100 +
.90
.80
.70
.60
.50
.40
.30
.20
.10
.0

DATE: ___/___/_____

#1 GOAL: _____

To-do list key: (fill in with colors/textures of your choosing, then complete box-chart!)
☐ started     ☐ finished     ☐ forgot     ☐ push to tomorrow

Tasks:
→

1.  2.  3.  4.  5.  6.  7.

a.m.

afternoon

p.m.

## FOOD DIARY:

BREAKFAST: _____

LUNCH: _____

DINNER: _____

SNACKS: _____

WATER (OZ/ML): _____

SPACE

"I have planted
**worth**
beneath my skin
in all the places
you made me
**doubt**."

-JADE EMMA WINDLE

Week of __/__/__ - __/__/__

GOAL FOR THE WEEK:

_____

Date: ___/___/_____

TODAY'S GOAL: _____

## To-do list:

FINISHED

.ALMOST

HALFWAY!

STARTED

. DIDN'T BEGIN

1  2  3  4  5  6

## Self-care Checklist:

☐ STAY HYDRATED
☐ EAT A HEALTHY BREAKFAST
☐ TAKE MEDS
☐ SPEND TIME IN NATURE
☐ SHOWER/BATHE
☐ EAT LOTS OF PLANTS
☐ READ
☐ EXERCISE
☐ RANDOM ACT OF KINDNESS
☐ ENJOY A HOT DRINK
☐ UNPLUG FOR AN HOUR
☐ YOGA/MEDITATION/MINDFULNESS

## Anxiety levels:

10
9
8
7
6
5
4
3
2
1

WAKE UP  A.M.  NOON  AFTERNOON  EVENING  BEDTIME

Date: ___/___/_____
TODAY'S GOAL: _____

TO DO LIST:

- 

- 

- 

SELF-CARE CHECKLIST

3 good things:

☐ STAY HYDRATED
☐ EAT A HEALTHY BREAKFAST          1.
☐ TAKE MEDS
☐ SPEND TIME IN NATURE
☐ SHOWER/BATHE                     2.
☐ EAT LOTS OF PLANTS
☐ READ
☐ EXERCISE
☐ RANDOM ACT OF KINDNESS           3.
☐ ENJOY A HOT DRINK
☐ UNPLUG FOR AN HOUR
☐ YOGA/MEDITATION/
   PRACTICE MINDFULNESS

Notes:

Date: ___/___/_____

To-do list:

○

○

○

Self-care checklist:

☐ STAY HYDRATED

☐ EAT A HEALTHY BREAKFAST

☐ TAKE MEDS

☐ SPEND TIME IN NATURE

☐ SHOWER/BATHE

☐ EAT LOTS OF PLANTS!

☐ READ

☐ EXERCISE

☐ RANDOM ACT OF KINDNESS

☐ UNPLUG FOR AN HOUR

☐ YOGA/MEDITATION

(WORK YOUR MAGIC)

**Date:** ___/___/_____

TODAY'S GOAL: _____

To Do List:

○

○

○

Mood Tracker:

AM:

Mid-Day:

PM:

Inspiring Quote: _____

SELF-CARE CHECKLIST:

☐ STAY HYDRATED
☐ EAT A HEALTHY BREAKFAST
☐ TAKE MEDS
☐ SPEND TIME IN NATURE
☐ SHOWER/BATHE
☐ EAT LOTS OF PLANTS
☐ READ
☐ EXERCISE
☐ RANDOM ACT OF KINDNESS
☐ ENJOY A HOT DRINK
☐ UNPLUG FOR AN HOUR
☐ YOGA/MEDITATION/MINDFULNES

HYDRATION LOG (WATER ONLY!)

Fluid ounces

100 +
.90
.80
.70
.60
.50
.40
.30
.20
.10
0

(don't forget a reusable bottle!)

DATE: ___ / ___ / _____

#1 GOAL: _____

| To-do list key: (fill in with colors/textures of your choosing, then complete box-chart!) |
| □ started      □ finished      □ forgot      □ push to tomorrow |

Tasks:
→

1.  2.  3.  4.  5.  6.  7.

a.m.

afternoon

p.m.

# FOOD DIARY:

BREAKFAST: _____

LUNCH: _____

DINNER: _____

SNACKS:_____

WATER (OZ/ML):_____

# S P A C E

"I will say it as many times
as it takes for you
to believe it:

you are **not** a burden."

-Chloë Frayne

Week of __/__/__ - __/__/__

GOAL FOR THE WEEK:
_____

Date: ___/___/_____

TODAY'S GOAL: _____

## To-do list:

| | | | | | |
|---|---|---|---|---|---|
FINISHED
.ALMOST
HALFWAY!
STARTED
.DIDN'T BEGIN

1  2  3  4  5  6

## Self-care Checklist:

☐ STAY HYDRATED
☐ EAT A HEALTHY BREAKFAST
☐ TAKE MEDS
☐ SPEND TIME IN NATURE
☐ SHOWER/BATHE
☐ EAT LOTS OF PLANTS
☐ READ
☐ EXERCISE
☐ RANDOM ACT OF KINDNESS
☐ ENJOY A HOT DRINK
☐ UNPLUG FOR AN HOUR
☐ YOGA/MEDITATION/MINDFULNESS

## Anxiety levels:

10
9
8
7
6
5
4
3
2
1

WAKE UP   A.M.   NOON   AFTERNOON   EVENING   BEDTIME

Date: ___/___/_____
TODAY'S GOAL: _____

TO DO LIST:

- 

- 

- 

SELF-CARE CHECKLIST

*3 good things:*

- ☐ STAY HYDRATED
- ☐ EAT A HEALTHY BREAKFAST
- ☐ TAKE MEDS
- ☐ SPEND TIME IN NATURE
- ☐ SHOWER/BATHE
- ☐ EAT LOTS OF PLANTS
- ☐ READ
- ☐ EXERCISE
- ☐ RANDOM ACT OF KINDNESS
- ☐ ENJOY A HOT DRINK
- ☐ UNPLUG FOR AN HOUR
- ☐ YOGA/MEDITATION/
   PRACTICE MINDFULNESS

1.

2.

3.

*Favorite places:*

Date: ___/___/_____

TODAY'S GOAL: _____

To-do list:

○

○

○

Self-care checklist:

☐ STAY HYDRATED
☐ EAT A HEALTHY BREAKFAST
☐ TAKE MEDS
☐ SPEND TIME IN NATURE
☐ SHOWER/BATHE
☐ EAT LOTS OF PLANTS!
☐ READ
☐ EXERCISE
☐ RANDOM ACT OF KINDNESS
☐ UNPLUG FOR AN HOUR
☐ YOGA/MEDITATION

(WORK YOUR MAGIC)

Date: ___/___/_____

TODAY'S GOAL: _____

Doodle something pretty:

## SELF-CARE CHECKLIST:

☐ STAY HYDRATED
☐ EAT A HEALTHY BREAKFAST
☐ TAKE MEDS
☐ SPEND TIME IN NATURE
☐ SHOWER/BATHE
☐ EAT LOTS OF PLANTS
☐ READ
☐ EXERCISE
☐ RANDOM ACT OF KINDNESS
☐ ENJOY A HOT DRINK
☐ UNPLUG FOR AN HOUR
☐ YOGA/MEDITATION/MINDFULNES

## HYDRATION LOG (WATER ONLY!)

Fluid ounces

100 +
.90
.80
.70
.60
.50
.40
.30
.20
.10
.0

DATE: ___/___/_____

#1 GOAL: _____

| To-do list key: (fill in with colors/textures of your choosing, then complete box-chart!) |
| □ started     □ finished     □ forgot     □ push to tomorrow |

Tasks:
→

1.  2.  3.  4.  5.  6.  7.

|  | | | | | | | | | | | | | | |
|---|---|---|---|---|---|---|---|---|---|---|---|---|---|---|
| a.m. | | | | | | | | | | | | | | |
| afternoon | | | | | | | | | | | | | | |
| p.m. | | | | | | | | | | | | | | |

# FOOD DIARY:

BREAKFAST: _____

LUNCH: _____

DINNER: _____

SNACKS: _____

WATER (OZ/ML): _____

# SPACE

"I AM NOT VERY *BRAVE,*
BUT I VERY MUCH TRY TO BE
AND I THINK THAT IS *ENOUGH*
FOR TODAY."

-Emily Byrnes

Week of __/__/__ - __/__/__

GOAL FOR THE WEEK:

_____

Date: ___/___/_____

TODAY'S GOAL: _____

## To-do list:

```
FINISHED
ALMOST
HALFWAY!
STARTED
DIDN'T BEGIN
```

1.   2.   3.   4.   5.   6.

## Self-care Checklist:

☐ STAY HYDRATED
☐ EAT A HEALTHY BREAKFAST
☐ TAKE MEDS
☐ SPEND TIME IN NATURE
☐ SHOWER/BATHE
☐ EAT LOTS OF PLANTS
☐ READ
☐ EXERCISE
☐ RANDOM ACT OF KINDNESS
☐ ENJOY A HOT DRINK
☐ UNPLUG FOR AN HOUR
☐ YOGA/MEDITATION/MINDFULNESS

## Anxiety levels:

```
10
9
8
7
6
5
4
3
2
1
   WAKE UP  A.M.  NOON  AFTERNOON  EVENING  BEDTIME
```

Date: ___/___/_____

TODAY'S GOAL: _____

TO DO LIST:

- 
- 
- 

SELF-CARE CHECKLIST

*3 good things:*

- ☐ STAY HYDRATED
- ☐ EAT A HEALTHY BREAKFAST
- ☐ TAKE MEDS
- ☐ SPEND TIME IN NATURE
- ☐ SHOWER/BATHE
- ☐ EAT LOTS OF PLANTS
- ☐ READ
- ☐ EXERCISE
- ☐ RANDOM ACT OF KINDNESS
- ☐ ENJOY A HOT DRINK
- ☐ UNPLUG FOR AN HOUR
- ☐ YOGA/MEDITATION/ PRACTICE MINDFULNESS

1.

2.

3.

*Books to read:*

Date: ___/___/_____

TODAY'S GOAL: _____

To-do list:

○

○

○

Self-care checklist:

- ☐ STAY HYDRATED
- ☐ EAT A HEALTHY BREAKFAST
- ☐ TAKE MEDS
- ☐ SPEND TIME IN NATURE
- ☐ SHOWER/BATHE
- ☐ EAT LOTS OF PLANTS!
- ☐ READ
- ☐ EXERCISE
- ☐ RANDOM ACT OF KINDNESS
- ☐ UNPLUG FOR AN HOUR
- ☐ YOGA/MEDITATION

(WORK YOUR MAGIC)

Date: ___/___/_____

TODAY'S GOAL: _____

To Do List:

○

○

○

Mood Tracker:

AM:

Mid-Day:

PM:

Inspiring Quote: _____
_____

## SELF-CARE CHECKLIST:

☐ STAY HYDRATED
☐ EAT A HEALTHY BREAKFAST
☐ TAKE MEDS
☐ SPEND TIME IN NATURE
☐ SHOWER/BATHE
☐ EAT LOTS OF PLANTS
☐ READ
☐ EXERCISE
☐ RANDOM ACT OF KINDNESS
☐ ENJOY A HOT DRINK
☐ UNPLUG FOR AN HOUR
☐ YOGA/MEDITATION/MINDFULNES

## HYDRATION LOG (WATER ONLY!)

fluid ounces

100 +
.90
.80
.70
.60
.50
.40
.30
.20
.10
0

(don't forget a reusable bottle!)

78

DATE: ___/___/_____

#1 GOAL: _____

To-do list key: (fill in with colors/textures of your choosing, then complete box-chart!)

☐ started ☐ finished ☐ forgot ☐ push to tomorrow

Tasks: →

| | 1. | 2. | 3. | 4. | 5. | 6. | 7. |
|---|---|---|---|---|---|---|---|
| a.m. | | | | | | | |
| afternoon | | | | | | | |
| p.m. | | | | | | | |

## FOOD DIARY:

BREAKFAST: _____

LUNCH: _____

DINNER: _____

SNACKS: _____

WATER (OZ/ML): _____

SPACE

"EVEN IN BROKEN MIRRORS
SHE SAW HER WORTH.
ONE THOUSAND
LITTLE PIECES
OF SELF-REFLECTION
REMINDING HER
HOW BEAUTIFULLY
SHE SURVIVED."

WILDER

Week of __/__/__ - __/__/__

GOAL FOR THE WEEK:

_____

Date: ___/___/_____

TODAY'S GOAL: _____

## To-do list:

FINISHED

.ALMOST

HALFWAY!

STARTED

.DIDN'T BEGIN

1.    2.    3.    4.    5.    6.

## Self-care Checklist:

☐ STAY HYDRATED
☐ EAT A HEALTHY BREAKFAST
☐ TAKE MEDS
☐ SPEND TIME IN NATURE
☐ SHOWER/BATHE
☐ EAT LOTS OF PLANTS
☐ READ
☐ EXERCISE
☐ RANDOM ACT OF KINDNESS
☐ ENJOY A HOT DRINK
☐ UNPLUG FOR AN HOUR
☐ YOGA/MEDITATION/MINDFULNESS

## Anxiety levels:

10
9
8
7
6
5
4
3
2
1

WAKE UP   A.M.   NOON   AFTERNOON   EVENING   BEDTIME

Date: ___/___/_____

TODAY'S GOAL: _____

TO DO LIST:

- 
- 
- 

## SELF-CARE CHECKLIST

*3 good things:*

- ☐ STAY HYDRATED
- ☐ EAT A HEALTHY BREAKFAST
- ☐ TAKE MEDS
- ☐ SPEND TIME IN NATURE
- ☐ SHOWER/BATHE
- ☐ EAT LOTS OF PLANTS
- ☐ READ
- ☐ EXERCISE
- ☐ RANDOM ACT OF KINDNESS
- ☐ ENJOY A HOT DRINK
- ☐ UNPLUG FOR AN HOUR
- ☐ YOGA/MEDITATION/
  PRACTICE MINDFULNESS

1.

2.

3.

*Places you've been:*

Date: ___/___/_____

TODAY'S GOAL: _____

To-do list:

o

o

o

Self-care checklist:

- ☐ STAY HYDRATED
- ☐ EAT A HEALTHY BREAKFAST
- ☐ TAKE MEDS
- ☐ SPEND TIME IN NATURE
- ☐ SHOWER/BATHE
- ☐ EAT LOTS OF PLANTS!
- ☐ READ
- ☐ EXERCISE
- ☐ RANDOM ACT OF KINDNESS
- ☐ UNPLUG FOR AN HOUR
- ☐ YOGA/MEDITATION

(WORK YOUR MAGIC)

Date: ___/___/_____

TODAY'S GOAL: _____

Doodle something pretty:

SELF-CARE CHECKLIST:

☐ STAY HYDRATED
☐ EAT A HEALTHY BREAKFAST
☐ TAKE MEDS
☐ SPEND TIME IN NATURE
☐ SHOWER/BATHE
☐ EAT LOTS OF PLANTS
☐ READ
☐ EXERCISE
☐ RANDOM ACT OF KINDNESS
☐ ENJOY A HOT DRINK
☐ UNPLUG FOR AN HOUR
☐ YOGA/MEDITATION/MINDFULNES

HYDRATION LOG (WATER ONLY!)

fluid ounces

100 +
90
80
70
60
50
40
30
20
10
0

(don't forget a reusable bottle!)

DATE: \_\_\_\_/\_\_\_\_/_____

#1 GOAL: _____

To-do list key: (fill in with colors/textures of your choosing, then complete box-chart!)

☐ started      ☐ finished      ☐ forgot      ☐ push to tomorrow

Tasks:

| | 1. | 2. | 3. | 4. | 5. | 6. | 7. |
|---|---|---|---|---|---|---|---|
| a.m. | | | | | | | |
| afternoon | | | | | | | |
| p.m. | | | | | | | |

# FOOD DIARY:

BREAKFAST: _____

LUNCH: _____

DINNER: _____

SNACKS:_____

WATER (OZ/ML):_____

# SPACE

"I MUST LEARN TO
FALL INTO OTHERS
WITHOUT FALLING OUT
OF MYSELF"

-EMILY BYRNES

Week of __/__/__ - __/__/__

GOAL FOR THE WEEK:

_____

Date: ___/___/_____

TODAY'S GOAL: _____

## To-do list:

FINISHED

.ALMOST

HALFWAY!

STARTED

. DIDN'T BEGIN

1  2  3  4  5  6

## Self-care Checklist:

☐ STAY HYDRATED
☐ EAT A HEALTHY BREAKFAST
☐ TAKE MEDS
☐ SPEND TIME IN NATURE
☐ SHOWER/BATHE
☐ EAT LOTS OF PLANTS
☐ READ
☐ EXERCISE
☐ RANDOM ACT OF KINDNESS
☐ ENJOY A HOT DRINK
☐ UNPLUG FOR AN HOUR
☐ YOGA/MEDITATION/MINDFULNESS

## Anxiety levels:

10
9
8
7
6
5
4
3
2
1

WAKE UP  A.M.  NOON  AFTERNOON  EVENING  BEDTIME

Date: ___/___/_____

TODAY'S GOAL: _____

TO DO LIST:

- 

- 

- 

SELF-CARE CHECKLIST                    3 good things:

☐ STAY HYDRATED
☐ EAT A HEALTHY BREAKFAST          1.
☐ TAKE MEDS
☐ SPEND TIME IN NATURE
☐ SHOWER/BATHE                     2.
☐ EAT LOTS OF PLANTS
☐ READ
☐ EXERCISE
☐ RANDOM ACT OF KINDNESS           3.
☐ ENJOY A HOT DRINK
☐ UNPLUG FOR AN HOUR
☐ YOGA/MEDITATION/
   PRACTICE MINDFULNESS

One thing you'd change about your life:

Date: \_\_\_/\_\_\_/_____

TODAY'S GOAL: _____

To-do list:

○

○

○

Self-care checklist:

☐ STAY HYDRATED

☐ EAT A HEALTHY BREAKFAST

☐ TAKE MEDS

☐ SPEND TIME IN NATURE

☐ SHOWER/BATHE

☐ EAT LOTS OF PLANTS!

☐ READ

☐ EXERCISE

☐ RANDOM ACT OF KINDNESS

☐ UNPLUG FOR AN HOUR

☐ YOGA/MEDITATION

(WORK YOUR MAGIC)

Date: ___/___/_____

TODAY'S GOAL: _____

To Do List:

○

○

○

Mood Tracker:

AM:

Mid-Day:

PM:

Inspiring Quote: _____

SELF-CARE CHECKLIST:

☐ STAY HYDRATED
☐ EAT A HEALTHY BREAKFAST
☐ TAKE MEDS
☐ SPEND TIME IN NATURE
☐ SHOWER/BATHE
☐ EAT LOTS OF PLANTS
☐ READ
☐ EXERCISE
☐ RANDOM ACT OF KINDNESS
☐ ENJOY A HOT DRINK
☐ UNPLUG FOR AN HOUR
☐ YOGA/MEDITATION/MINDFULNES

HYDRATION LOG (WATER ONLY!)

Fluid ounces

100 +
.90
.80
.70
.60
.50
.40
.30
.20
.10
0

(don't forget a reusable bottle!)

DATE: ____/____/_____

#1 GOAL: _____

| To-do list key: (fill in with colors/textures of your choosing, then complete box-chart!) |
|---|
| □ started    □ finished    □ forgot    □ push to tomorrow |

Tasks: →

1.    2.    3.    4.    5.    6.    7.

|  | | | | | | | | | | | | | | |
|---|---|---|---|---|---|---|---|---|---|---|---|---|---|---|
| a.m. | | | | | | | | | | | | | | |
| afternoon | | | | | | | | | | | | | | |
| p.m. | | | | | | | | | | | | | | |

# FOOD DIARY:

BREAKFAST: _____

LUNCH: _____

DINNER: _____

SNACKS: _____

WATER (OZ/ML): _____

# S P A C E

"A SUNFLOWER

IS STILL A SUNFLOWER

EVEN WHEN IT ISN'T

FACING THE SUN."

-ALANNAH RADBURN

Week of __/__/__ - __/__/__

GOAL FOR THE WEEK:

_____

Date: ___/___/_____

TODAY'S GOAL: _____

# To-do list:

FINISHED

.ALMOST

HALFWAY!

STARTED

.DIDN'T BEGIN

1.   2.   3.   4.   5.   6.

# Self-care Checklist:

☐ STAY HYDRATED
☐ EAT A HEALTHY BREAKFAST
☐ TAKE MEDS
☐ SPEND TIME IN NATURE
☐ SHOWER/BATHE
☐ EAT LOTS OF PLANTS
☐ READ
☐ EXERCISE
☐ RANDOM ACT OF KINDNESS
☐ ENJOY A HOT DRINK
☐ UNPLUG FOR AN HOUR
☐ YOGA/MEDITATION/MINDFULNESS

# Anxiety levels:

10
9
8
7
6
5
4
3
2
1

WAKE UP   A.M.   NOON   AFTERNOON   EVENING   BEDTIME

**Date: ___/___/_____**

TODAY'S GOAL: _____

## TO DO LIST:

- 
- 
- 

## SELF-CARE CHECKLIST

*3 good things:*

☐ STAY HYDRATED
☐ EAT A HEALTHY BREAKFAST          1.
☐ TAKE MEDS
☐ SPEND TIME IN NATURE
☐ SHOWER/BATHE                     2.
☐ EAT LOTS OF PLANTS
☐ READ
☐ EXERCISE
☐ RANDOM ACT OF KINDNESS           3.
☐ ENJOY A HOT DRINK
☐ UNPLUG FOR AN HOUR
☐ YOGA/MEDITATION/
   PRACTICE MINDFULNESS

*Things you're thankful for:*

Date: ___/___/_____

TODAY'S GOAL: _____

To-do list:

    ○

    ○

    ○

Self-care checklist:

☐ STAY HYDRATED

☐ EAT A HEALTHY BREAKFAST

☐ TAKE MEDS

☐ SPEND TIME IN NATURE

☐ SHOWER/BATHE

☐ EAT LOTS OF PLANTS!

☐ READ

☐ EXERCISE

☐ RANDOM ACT OF KINDNESS

☐ UNPLUG FOR AN HOUR

☐ YOGA/MEDITATION

(WORK YOUR MAGIC)

Date: ___/___/_____

TODAY'S GOAL: _____

Doodle something pretty:

## SELF-CARE CHECKLIST:

☐ STAY HYDRATED
☐ EAT A HEALTHY BREAKFAST
☐ TAKE MEDS
☐ SPEND TIME IN NATURE
☐ SHOWER/BATHE
☐ EAT LOTS OF PLANTS
☐ READ
☐ EXERCISE
☐ RANDOM ACT OF KINDNESS
☐ ENJOY A HOT DRINK
☐ UNPLUG FOR AN HOUR
☐ YOGA/MEDITATION/MINDFULNES

## HYDRATION LOG (WATER ONLY!)

Fluid ounces

100 +
.90
.80
.70
.60
.50
.40
.30
.20
.10
0

DATE: ____ / ____ / _____

#1 GOAL: _____

Tasks: →

1.   2.   3.   4.   5.   6.   7.

| | | | | | | | | | | | | | |
|---|---|---|---|---|---|---|---|---|---|---|---|---|---|
| a.m. | | | | | | | | | | | | | |
| afternoon | | | | | | | | | | | | | |
| p.m. | | | | | | | | | | | | | |

# FOOD DIARY:

BREAKFAST: _____

LUNCH: _____

DINNER: _____

SNACKS: _____

WATER (OZ/ML): _____

# SPACE

Not everyone is meant to stay,
and *that's okay.*

-Salma El-Wardany

Week of __/__/__ - __/__/__

GOAL FOR THE WEEK:

_____

Date: ___/___/_____

TODAY'S GOAL: _____

# To-do list:

FINISHED

.ALMOST

HALFWAY!

STARTED

. DIDN'T BEGIN

1.
2.
3.
4.
5.
6.

## Self-care Checklist:

☐ STAY HYDRATED
☐ EAT A HEALTHY BREAKFAST
☐ TAKE MEDS
☐ SPEND TIME IN NATURE
☐ SHOWER/BATHE
☐ EAT LOTS OF PLANTS
☐ READ
☐ EXERCISE
☐ RANDOM ACT OF KINDNESS
☐ ENJOY A HOT DRINK
☐ UNPLUG FOR AN HOUR
☐ YOGA/MEDITATION/MINDFULNESS

## Anxiety levels:

10
9
8
7
6
5
4
3
2
1

WAKE UP
-A.M.
NOON
AFTERNOON
EVENING
BEDTIME

Date: ___/___/_____

TODAY'S GOAL: _____

## TO DO LIST:

- 
- 
- 

## SELF-CARE CHECKLIST

*3 good things:*

- ☐ STAY HYDRATED
- ☐ EAT A HEALTHY BREAKFAST
- ☐ TAKE MEDS
- ☐ SPEND TIME IN NATURE
- ☐ SHOWER/BATHE
- ☐ EAT LOTS OF PLANTS
- ☐ READ
- ☐ EXERCISE
- ☐ RANDOM ACT OF KINDNESS
- ☐ ENJOY A HOT DRINK
- ☐ UNPLUG FOR AN HOUR
- ☐ YOGA/MEDITATION/
  PRACTICE MINDFULNESS

1.

2.

3.

*You're stuck on a desert island. What 5 books do you bring?*

Date: ___/___/_____

TODAY'S GOAL: _____

To-do list:

○

○

○

Self-care checklist:

☐ STAY HYDRATED

☐ EAT A HEALTHY BREAKFAST

☐ TAKE MEDS

☐ SPEND TIME IN NATURE

☐ SHOWER/BATHE

☐ EAT LOTS OF PLANTS!

☐ READ

☐ EXERCISE

☐ RANDOM ACT OF KINDNESS

☐ UNPLUG FOR AN HOUR

☐ YOGA/MEDITATION

(WORK YOUR MAGIC)

Date: ___/___/_____

TODAY'S GOAL: _____

To Do List:

○

○

○

Mood Tracker:

AM:

Mid-Day:

PM:

Inspiring Quote: _____
_____

SELF-CARE CHECKLIST:

☐ STAY HYDRATED
☐ EAT A HEALTHY BREAKFAST
☐ TAKE MEDS
☐ SPEND TIME IN NATURE
☐ SHOWER/BATHE
☐ EAT LOTS OF PLANTS
☐ READ
☐ EXERCISE
☐ RANDOM ACT OF KINDNESS
☐ ENJOY A HOT DRINK
☐ UNPLUG FOR AN HOUR
☐ YOGA/MEDITATION/MINDFULNESS

HYDRATION LOG (WATER ONLY!)

Fluid ounces

100 +
.90
.80
.70
.60
.50
.40
.30
.20
.10
0

(don't forget a reusable bottle!)

DATE: ____/____/_____

#1 GOAL: _____

| To-do list key: (fill in with colors/textures of your choosing, then complete box-chart!) |
| --- |
| ☐ started      ☐ finished      ☐ forgot      ☐ push to tomorrow |

Tasks: →

1.  2.  3.  4.  5.  6.  7.

| | a.m. | | | | | | | | | | | |
| --- | --- | --- | --- | --- | --- | --- | --- | --- | --- | --- | --- | --- |
| afternoon | | | | | | | | | | | | |
| p.m. | | | | | | | | | | | | |

# FOOD DIARY:

BREAKFAST: _____

LUNCH: _____

DINNER: _____

SNACKS: _____

WATER (OZ/ML):_____

# SPACE

# P.S. YOU'VE GOT THIS

Contributors and where to find them:

Alannah Radburn
Instagram: @alannahradburn.poetry
Book: *Yellow, Excerpts from my Exorcism*

A.N. Moore
Instagram: @anmooreword
Book: *Love Will Find You Elsewhere*

Chloë Frayne
Instagram: @chloefrayne
Books: *Into Oblivion, Letters and Why They're All for You*

Jade Emma Windle
Instagram: @shipswithsails

Leah J. Stone
Instagram: @leahjstone
Book: *Dig Yourself Up*

r.iver
Instagram: @rogueonme

Salma El-Wardany
Instagram: @salmaelwardany

Wilder
Instagram: @wilderpoetry
Books: *Wild is She, Nocturnal*

# FOLLOW ON INSTAGRAM: @BY.EMILYBYRNES

## (FACEBOOK AND TWITTER, TOO)

Everything by Emily Byrnes can be found on Amazon.com worldwide as well as other online retailers and choice small businesses. Please leave a review if you find something you love, and thank you for supporting independent writers. <3

Made in the USA
Columbia, SC
26 November 2019

83843429R00109